# GREAT CANADIANS

# Entrepreneurs

**Shaun Hunter**

# Weigl

CALGARY

www.weigl.com

## Dedication

*This series is dedicated to all Canadians who take pride in their communities and their citizenship; and to those who will continue to help build a strong Canada. The Canadians in this series have helped to build Canada by being outstanding in their fields, from literature to business, sports to the arts. Some have overcome great obstacles to make their dreams come true, and their dedication and achievement serve as an inspiration for young and old alike.*

Published by Weigl Educational Publishers Limited
6325-10 Street SE
Calgary, Alberta, Canada
T2H 2Z9
Web site: http://www.weigl.com
Copyright © 2000 WEIGL EDUCATIONAL PUBLISHERS LIMITED

Canadian Cataloguing in Publication Data

Hunter, Shaun, 1961–
Entrepreneurs

(Great Canadians)
Includes bibliographical references and index.
ISBN 1-896990-09-6

1. Businesspeople—Canada—Biography—Juvenile literature. I. Title. II. Series:
Great Canadians (Calgary, Alta.)
HC112.5.A2H86 1999            j338'.04'092271            C99-910535-3

Printed in Canada
1 2 3 4 5 6 7 8 9 0   03 20 01 00 99

**Editor**
Leslie Strudwick
**Design**
Warren Clark
**Cover Design**
Chris Bowerman
**Copy Editor**
Rennay Craats
**Layout**
Lucinda Cage

## Photograph Credits

Every reasonable effort has been made to trace ownership and to obtain permission to reprint copyright material. The publishers would be pleased to have any errors or omissions brought to their attention so that they may be corrected in subsequent printings.

Archive Photos: pages 11, 12, 15, 23; Courtesy The Bata Shoe Museum: page 6; Courtesy Carleton University: page 13; Courtesy Wayne Clark: page 42; CP Picture Archive: pages 14, 17, 18, 20, 21, 22, 29, 34, 35; Courtesy Harrison McCain: pages 24, 25, 27, 28; Courtesy Wallace McCain: page 26; Courtesy Jack McClelland: page 43; Courtesy Umberto Menghi: page 44; Courtesy Moriyama and Teshima: page 10; National Archives: page 8; Courtesy *Saturday Night* magazine: page 16; Courtesy Ron and Marg Southern: page 45; Courtesy Lise Watier: pages 30, 31, 32, 33; Courtesy Moses Znaimer: cover, pages: 36, 38, 39, 40, 41.

# CONTENTS

# Entrepreneurs

What does it take to be a leader in business? One way to define a business leader is to look at financial success. Successful businesspeople make money for their company. They are able to make tough decisions. They have the confidence and respect of the people around them. They are good judges of risk. Business leaders can also be good citizens who help their communities and their country.

Business has been conducted in Canada for centuries. The early European settlers set up one of Canada's most well-known businesses, the Hudson's Bay Company, which still exists across the country. Today, Canadians are involved in many different kinds of business. Their places of business span the world. Some are **entrepreneurs** who start businesses from scratch. Others inherit family businesses and must continue to develop markets for their products and services.

The Canadians profiled in this book are only a few of the many successful businesspeople in Canada. You may know some of their names or the products their companies make. The people in this book are involved in different kinds of business, but they share many qualities. Many of them have been awarded one of the country's highest honours, the Order of Canada.

Each of the people featured in this book has taken a different road to business success. The major profiles look at six Canadian business leaders in detail. The stories of their lives reveal how they started in business, their challenges, and their accomplishments. The last section of the book gives brief descriptions of other successful Canadian businesspeople whose stories you may wish to explore further.

*1926—*

# Sonja Bata

> **" Business is about how to serve your customers and how to help your employees improve their own knowledge and skills and, because of it, have a better quality of life. "**

## Key Events

**1946** Marries Thomas Bata

**1965** Becomes a director of the Bata Shoe Organization

**1982** Receives the silver medal in the United Nations Environmental Program

**1983** Becomes an Officer of the Order of Canada

**1983–85** Chairs the World Wildlife Fund Canada

**1991** Is inducted into the Canadian Business Hall of Fame

**1995** Opens the Bata Shoe Museum in Toronto

# Early Years

Sonja Wettstein grew up in Zurich, Switzerland. When she was three years old, she met Thomas Bata. Thomas's father owned a successful shoemaking business in Czechoslovakia. He had taken his son on a business trip to meet with Sonja's father, a lawyer. At the time, Sonja did not pay much attention to the fifteen-year-old boy from Czechoslovakia.

Sonja's parents encouraged her to do well at school. They also told her that it was important to make a contribution to society. Her father had helped start the International Red Cross and the Rotarian service clubs. Sonja wanted to become a famous architect. She studied architecture in Zurich. While she was at school, Sonja met Thomas again. Her career plans changed when Thomas asked her to marry him. Flying above the Swiss Alps in Thomas's airplane, Sonja decided to marry this dynamic businessman.

Sonja's mother thought that her daughter did not have the skills to run a household. A few months before the wedding, Sonja took a crash course in keeping house. At that time, no one knew the important role she would play in the Bata shoe business.

> ❝ *I was brought up by parents who [taught] us from early childhood that we had to do something worthwhile in life.* ❞

Czechoslovakia is now two separate countries: the Czech Republic and Slovakia.

## Backgrounder

### The Bata Shoemakers

Many of Thomas Bata's ancestors had been shoemakers in Moravia, now part of the Czech Republic. Thomas's father built a thriving shoe business in the tiny village of Zlin. He exported shoes throughout the world. Thomas started out as an apprentice in his father's business. Eventually, he became a manager. World War II struck a harsh blow to Bata Shoes. In 1939, the Nazis took over Czechoslovakia. Then in 1945, the communists came to power and took control of the company. Thomas had to rebuild the business abroad.

# Developing Skills

Soon after they married, Sonja and Thomas moved to a village in central Ontario. Thomas had come to Canada a few years before, when the Nazis took over Czechoslovakia in 1939. In Ontario, he had started his family's shoe business. Sonja and Thomas set up house in a small cottage near the Bata factory. Very quickly, Sonja realized she was not well-suited for life as a housewife. Thomas was hard at work trying to rebuild his father's shoe business after the war. Sonja decided to work with Thomas. With her training in architecture and her interest in design, she wanted to help Thomas modernize the company.

Sonja had many fresh ideas about new designs the company could produce. Armed with samples, Sonja visited several Bata managers. They greeted her politely, but they ignored her ideas. Managers were not eager to use Sonja's designs. She was young, a newcomer, and the boss's wife. They did not think she understood the shoe business as well as they did.

> *During the first twenty to thirty years of our marriage, the business dominated our private lives. The business was the biggest child.*

Soon after Sonja married Thomas, she decided to help him run the Bata shoe business.

Sonja was frustrated by the lack of enthusiasm for her ideas. Thomas suggested she learn more about the business. Sonja jumped at the chance to work in a company store in London, England. For several weeks, Sonja did everything from fitting and selling shoes to stocktaking, ordering, accounting, and hiring. She also took courses in shoe design and pattern cutting.

*" I find it disturbing that the traditional ways of shoemaking are dying out. "*

During the first ten years of their marriage, Sonja and Thomas travelled around the world to visit Bata factories. These were years of rapid growth. New factories were built in India, Africa, and South America. Together, the Batas made speeches, showed their samples, and gave presentations. They learned about the needs and tastes of people in each country. Sonja was most interested in developing and marketing products in different parts of the world. Sonja and Thomas discussed business plans and challenges.

Bata shoe stores can be found around the world.

# Backgrounder

## Batawa

During World War II, Thomas opened a new Canadian factory near Trenton, Ontario. He arranged for 250 Bata workers from Czechoslovakia to settle in Ontario with their families. He moved hundreds of machines from his Czech factory. On farmland surrounding the new factory, Bata built homes for company employees. Thomas called the new community Batawa, combining the company name and the last syllable of the word Ottawa. There are two more Bata towns, one in India and the other in France.

# Accomplishments

As Sonja gained experience and knowledge, the Bata company adopted her ideas. She helped improve the image of Bata stores through better window displays and advertising. Sonja designed a model for a standard Bata shoe store to be used around the world. The furniture, carpet, and shelves for each store were packed as a portable kit. This meant that new Bata stores could be put together quickly. Sonja worked with architects who were building new factories. She also told managers of a radical new trend in women's footwear, shoes with pointed toes. Sonja's advice caused the company to change its machinery to fit the new design.

The Batas were very successful in rebuilding the business. They took a company that had been crippled during World War II and made it into a profitable international business. At its height, Bata Shoes made footwear in sixty-four factories in sixty-one countries. In 1995, Bata sold more than 300 million shoes. Sonja is proud of the company's role in developing countries. She believes that Bata Shoes improved the standard of living for many people in these areas. Bata created jobs, provided training and education, and introduced modern technology.

▶▶▶▶▶▶

## Quick Notes

▶ Sonja has donated her time and expertise to groups involving young people. She has worked with Junior Achievement of Canada and the Girl Guide World Association.

▶ In 1989, Sonja was made an honorary captain in the Canadian navy.

▶ Sonja has four children. The Bata children frequently accompanied their parents on business trips.

▶ Sonja wanted the Bata Shoe Museum to have a coat of arms. The museum's motto is "One step at a time."

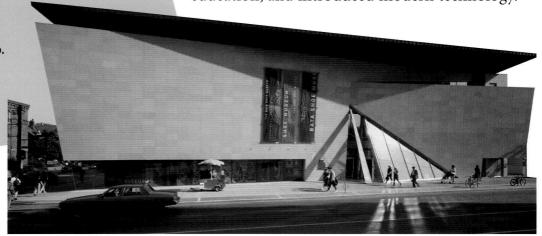

The Bata Shoe Museum is in Toronto, Ontario.

> " *No artifact tells you more about people than a pair of shoes. Shoes tell us about their way of life, their status in society, the climate in which they lived, their activities, and sometimes even their religious beliefs.* "

Sonja's interests in architecture, design, and the arts have led her to donate her time and expertise to non-profit groups. In the 1970s, she headed the National Design Council. This group looks at the effects of good design on people and their environments. Sonja has also been a director of the Art Gallery of Ontario. She has worked for many years with the World Wildlife Fund. This group helps to protect endangered species. Through her travels with Bata shoes, Sonja learned about many of the countries facing **ecological** challenges.

Sonja holds Elton John's famous platform boots from the 1970s. She is in part of the Bata Shoe Museum that displays shoemaking tools from the eighteenth century.

In Sonja's first years with Bata, she became fascinated by the history of shoes. During her fifty-year career, Sonja has collected more than 10,000 pairs of shoes. In 1995, she opened the Bata Shoe Museum in Toronto. The museum features the shoes of famous people such as Madonna and Elton John. It also displays shoes from many countries and periods of history. The Bata Shoe Museum combines Sonja's passions for design, the arts, education, and footwear.

# Backgrounder

## The Bata Shoe Museum

When Sonja travelled the world on business, she would often meet people wearing interesting shoes. She would ask if she could have the shoes, and in exchange, buy that person a new pair. In the late 1970s, Sonja could no longer store her huge collection of shoes from around the world. She decided to open a museum. The museum building was inspired by the shape of a shoe box with the roof like a lid resting on the box. The museum's exhibits have included the role of shoes in children's stories and the Inuit art of making boots.

# 1944–

# Conrad Black

> ❝ Never bet more than you can afford to lose. No matter how enticing the prize is, don't do it. ❞

## Key Events

**1966** Becomes editor and publisher of a small newspaper in rural Quebec

**1969** Begins buying small English-language newspapers in Quebec

**1977** Publishes a book on Quebec politician Maurice Duplessis

**1978** Takes control of the Argus Corporation; is named Man of the Year by *Report on Business*

**1986** Buys shares in London's *Daily Telegraph*

**1989** Becomes the chief executive officer of the *Daily Telegraph*

**1990** Becomes a member of the Order of Canada

**1992** Organizes a takeover of Southam, a large Canadian newspaper company

**1993** Publishes his autobiography, *A Life in Progress*

**1998** Launches a new national Canadian newspaper, *The National Post*

# Early Years

**C**onrad was just one year old when his family moved from Montreal to Toronto. The Black family later bought a home in what was then the outskirts of Toronto. Conrad was a thin boy with a shock of red hair. Conrad liked to spend time by himself. He loved to read and especially liked books about the military. He also liked listening to recordings of speeches by political leaders.

Conrad was a bright child with a large vocabulary and an excellent memory. When he was twelve, he could recite statistics about warships, world leaders, and sports. In spite of his intelligence, Conrad did poorly in school. He was expelled from two private boys' schools.

Conrad scraped through and finished high school. He studied journalism at Carleton University in Ottawa. After one term, he switched to history. During his student years, he lived in an old hotel in Ottawa. There, he played cards with the politicians who also lived at the hotel.

> " *We didn't suddenly sit down one day and decide we would become media tycoons.* "

The journalism program at Carleton University is widely respected.

## **B**ackgrounder

### Father and Son

Conrad was very close to his father. As a boy, he often listened to his father talk about business. George Black had **investments** in a company called Argus. Argus was run by some of the top businesspeople in the country, including E.P. Taylor and Bud McDougald. Argus was a holding company. It did not do business itself, but invested in other businesses. Conrad listened carefully to his father's stories. When he was seven, he decided that one day he would become head of Argus.

# Developing Skills

**W**hile he was at university, Conrad took a trip to Europe. He became interested in world affairs. He also became fascinated by William Randolph Hearst, an American who owned newspapers. After failing his first year at law school, Conrad had to decide what to do next. A friend offered him a job at a small newspaper in Quebec. Conrad took the job and started his career in the newspaper business. He learned all about the paper, from layout, circulation, and advertising, to writing. After six months, Conrad had turned the paper into a profitable business. Soon, he and two friends bought another small Quebec newspaper. They quickly made it profitable. The trio called their business Sterling Newspapers.

> **❝** *I want to build a first-class international newspaper company, and I think the omens are favourable.* **❞**

During his years in Quebec, Conrad learned how to speak French. He also became interested in the life of Maurice Duplessis, a former premier of Quebec. During the day, Conrad helped to run the newspaper business. At night, he researched and wrote about Duplessis. His apartment was crammed with letters and documents. In 1977, he published a biography of Duplessis. Conrad's book received strong reviews as an important study on this man. The book showed that Conrad was a serious and capable historian.

Conrad was intrigued by former Quebec premier Maurice Duplessis.

## **B**ackgrounder

### Maurice Duplessis

Duplessis was premier of Quebec for eighteen years, between 1936 and 1959. He was a colourful man and a powerful leader. His government carried out huge projects such as building highways, hospitals, and schools, and developing the hydroelectric system. During the Duplessis years, Quebec was a growing and prosperous province.

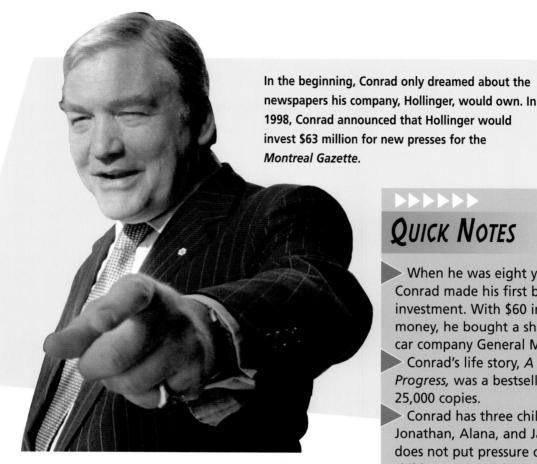

In the beginning, Conrad only dreamed about the newspapers his company, Hollinger, would own. In 1998, Conrad announced that Hollinger would invest $63 million for new presses for the *Montreal Gazette*.

▷▷▷▷▷▷

## QUICK NOTES

▷ When he was eight years old, Conrad made his first business investment. With $60 in saved money, he bought a share in the car company General Motors.

▷ Conrad's life story, *A Life in Progress,* was a bestseller. It sold 25,000 copies.

▷ Conrad has three children, Jonathan, Alana, and James. He does not put pressure on his children to join his business. Instead, he encourages them to follow their own dreams.

▷ As a child, Conrad was fascinated by ships. As an adult, he has built a collection of model battleships, which he displays in glass cases in his Toronto home.

▷ Conrad had a coat of arms created for his Toronto property. The design features a book, an eagle, a **plumb** line to represent his roots overseas, wheat sheaves for western Canada, and a fleur-de-lis for Quebec.

A few years before his book came out, Conrad went back to Toronto. He started working in his father's business. This business controlled much of the Argus Corporation. When one of the founders of Argus passed away, Conrad jumped in. Conrad and his brother eventually took control of Argus. For the next few years, Conrad looked at the companies Argus controlled. He let go of companies that were losing money and added companies that were profitable.

Eventually, Conrad bought out his Argus partners. He started building a new business called Hollinger. Hollinger's focus was newspapers. Over the years, Conrad and his two friends at Sterling Newspapers had bought papers in western Canada and the Maritimes. These papers were now controlled by Hollinger.

# Accomplishments

In 1985, Conrad learned that a respected British newspaper was losing money. Conrad had often read the *Daily Telegraph*. He admired the paper. Conrad's first investment in the *Telegraph* was small. A few months later, the newspaper needed more help. Conrad bought a large part of the newspaper and turned it around. By 1990, the *Telegraph* was one of the most profitable and widely read newspapers in Britain.

The *Telegraph's* success allowed Conrad to buy other newspapers. Between 1986 and 1992, Conrad's company spent $300 million for 288 newspapers. Many of these were small papers in Canada and the United States. Conrad also bought newspapers in Australia and Israel.

His international business was growing, but Conrad also owned many papers in Canada. He wanted to add to Hollinger's small newspapers. In 1987, he bought a large newspaper company in Quebec. That same year, Conrad bought *Saturday Night* magazine. Conrad liked the literary and political focus of this established Canadian magazine. In 1992, Conrad helped to take over Southam. It owned newspapers in many Canadian cities. In 1998, Conrad led Southam in starting a new national newspaper, *The National Post*.

> " I feel myself very fortunate. I have a position perfectly suited for me that I've worked rather hard for a number of years to design. I do pretty much what I like and don't do very much that I don't like.... I'm personally happy with my lot. "

Conrad took over ownership of *Saturday Night* magazine in 1987.

**Conrad holds one of the many newspapers that he owns, the *Financial Post*.**

Conrad always made time for writing in his busy life. For a while, he wrote a column in a business magazine. Conrad wrote about his opinions on politics, religion, business, and even sports. One of his favourite topics was the relations between French- and English-speaking Canada. Many people talked about his views.

Conrad had been well-known since his takeover of Argus in 1978. A few people applauded his success, but many criticized him. His way of doing business and his political beliefs made some people angry. The media often wrote about Conrad. He was a rich man. He had a high-flying lifestyle, jetting between Toronto, London, and New York City. His friends included many famous people. Conrad wanted to tell his own story. In 1993, he wrote his autobiography, *A Life in Progress.* The book explains how he has succeeded in building an international newspaper company. Today, Conrad's publishing empire is the third largest in the world.

# **B**ackgrounder

## The *National Post*

On October 27, 1998, the first edition of the *National Post* hit Canadian streets. By noon, the paper had sold out in many places. The *National Post* covers Canadian and international news, business, sports, and entertainment six days a week. The weekend edition includes feature stories and opinion pieces. The *Post's* editors want the new paper to be a powerful voice. The *National Post* competes directly for readers with some of Canada's largest daily newspapers.

*1937–*

# George Cohon

> **Persistence and determination are part of my life. It gets my back up if you say I can't do something.**

## Key Events

**1961** Graduates from Northwestern University law school in Chicago

**1967** Gives up his law practice and obtains rights to McDonald's restaurants in eastern Canada

**1975** Becomes a Canadian citizen

**1976** Sets his sights on introducing McDonald's to the Soviet Union

**1981** Receives Israel's highest public service award, the Israel Prime Minister Medal

**1987** Becomes a Member of the Order of Canada

**1990** McDonald's opens its first restaurant in the former Soviet Union

**1993** Becomes an Officer of the Order of Canada

**1997** Publishes his autobiography, *To Russia with Fries*

**1998** Is inducted into the Canadian Business Hall of Fame

# Early Years

George grew up on the south side of Chicago. During his childhood, south Chicago was a lively community of Jewish, Irish, and Italian immigrants. George's grandparents had settled in the area in the early 1900s. They had moved to the United States to escape the pogroms, the killing of Jewish people in Ukraine.

When George was growing up, his father ran the family's small bakery. George started working when he was eleven. He counted bolts and washers at his grandfather's plumbing store. Later on, he worked as a shoe salesman and a door-to-door salesman. George went to university and then law school in Chicago. He married and started work in a small law firm. For the next few years, George settled into the busy life of a lawyer and father of two young sons.

One day, George's life changed direction. He had been helping a client start a McDonald's restaurant. The client decided not to go ahead. Suddenly, George had a chance to buy the rights to McDonald's restaurants in eastern Canada. He already knew he did not want to be a lawyer for the rest of his life.

George's grandparents moved to the United States to escape danger in the Ukraine.

Sweden

Finland

Estonia

Latvia

Lithuania

Poland

Belarus

Russia

Ukraine

Romania

Kazakhstan

## Backgrounder

### The Pogroms

During the late 1800s, European attitudes toward Jews were very negative. Poland and Russia had previously left Jewish people alone, but these countries became actively involved in **anti-semitism**. People in Russia and some of the surrounding countries began killing thousands of Jews in a series of massacres called pogroms. About 2 million Jewish people fled from the region. Some went to the United States and others moved to Palestine in the Middle East, which would later become Israel.

# Developing Skills

In 1967, George invested all his savings and borrowed money from his family and friends to start his new business. He quickly set off for Toronto. In Canada, fast-food restaurants were just becoming popular. Most people had not heard of McDonald's. The competition between fast-food companies became fierce. To start his business, George had to work very hard. He travelled all over Ontario to meet with people and tour possible sites. He gave hundreds of speeches to community groups to get the McDonald's name known. In 1968, George opened his first McDonald's restaurant, in London, Ontario.

Every year, George and his team opened more restaurants. In four years, he had opened thirty-four McDonald's restaurants east of Manitoba. In 1971, he became the president of McDonald's Restaurants of Canada. George was making McDonald's restaurants well-known across the country.

In the mid-1970s, George began to look beyond Canada. He was convinced that McDonald's could do business in the Soviet Union. People thought George's dream was impossible and crazy. The Soviet Union and western countries were still engaged in the **Cold War**, a power struggle between communist and western countries. The Soviet Union did not want companies from the West doing business inside its borders.

The first McDonald's outside of the United States was in Canada. George helped open McDonald's restaurants across Canada.

“ *If there's a space station and docking, and 10,000 people, there should be a McDonald's (on Mars). You bet.* ”

**George introduced the Soviet ambassador to Canada, Alexi Rodinov, to his first Big Mac.**

In 1976, George and his family were in Montreal to see the Olympic Games. They bumped into a Soviet **delegation** and offered to take them to a nearby McDonald's restaurant. The Soviets had never seen such a place. George asked them if they thought people would go to a McDonald's in the Soviet Union. They quickly replied, "Yes!" Later, George could not stop thinking about it. He started to wonder if McDonald's could provide food to athletes at the next Olympic Games in Moscow in 1980.

During the next two or three years, George travelled to Moscow often. He met with officials and talked to ordinary citizens. In George's mind, the Olympics was a way for McDonald's to get into the Soviet Union. George was looking ahead to the time when McDonald's would set up restaurants all over the Soviet Union. Back home, many believed he was wasting his time. It was too hard to do business in the Soviet Union. Right before the Olympics was to begin, the deal that George had worked so hard for fell through.

# Backgrounder

## Politics and the Olympic Games in Moscow

In 1979, the Soviet Union invaded Afghanistan to fight people who were against communism. To protest the invasion, the United States did not allow its athletes to take part in the 1980 Olympic Games in Moscow. Many other western countries, including Canada, joined the boycott. The boycott took place during a power struggle between the United States and the Soviet Union that dated back to the 1950s.

# Accomplishments

George was disappointed when the Olympic deal fell through. But he did not give up. He knew that the Soviet Union could be a huge market for McDonald's.

In the early 1980s, George started to negotiate with the Soviets again. He even had to explain what a hamburger was. As George worked on his plan, he noticed that Soviet society was slowly starting to change. Most citizens were poor. Many were frustrated by their lack of freedom. New Soviet policies of **glasnost** and **perestroika** were starting to take hold.

In 1989, after thirteen years of talking, the Soviets finally agreed. However, George had to guarantee that McDonald's in Moscow would serve exactly the same food and run as well as McDonald's in Canada. In Canada, McDonald's bought supplies such as buns, meat, and milk from independent companies. In the Soviet Union, local suppliers could not meet these standards. McDonald's set up its own supply company close to Moscow to process the local goods. George and his team built a huge factory, trained 400 people to work there, and introduced new technology.

Some of the people that were going to work at McDonald's in Moscow were flown to Toronto to learn how to make hamburgers.

# Backgrounder

## The Opening of Soviet Society

In the 1980s, Soviet president Mikhail Gorbachev introduced new ideas that changed Soviet society. *Glasnost* and *perestroika* loosened government controls on the Soviet people. Soviets were allowed more freedom. The government also changed its attitudes toward western countries and slowly welcomed back people who had left for other countries. *Glasnost* and *perestroika* led to the breaking up of the Soviet Union in 1991. The country divided into a number of smaller, independent states.

> When people said, 'You'll never find the staff.' I always thought, Excuse me, who wins the Olympics all the time? Do you mean to tell me that people who learn how to win gold medals are incapable of learning how to make a hamburger?

In 1998, George received the Order of Friendship from Russian president Boris Yeltsin.

The first McDonald's in the Soviet Union opened in January, 1990, in Moscow. George called the opening day one of the most important days in his life. When the doors opened, Soviets flocked to the counter to taste their first hamburgers. Reporters and television cameras from around the world came to record the event. The Moscow restaurant, with 700 seats, was the largest in the world. George's instincts about doing business in the Soviet Union were right. By the end of 1998, forty-six McDonald's restaurants in twelve Russian cities had opened. Former Soviet president Mikhail Gorbachev believed George's success was an important step in building a new society in the Soviet Union.

Today, George is a top businessperson. His personality makes him a strong leader. He has a sense of adventure and finds risk exciting. George also has an interest in giving back to the community. He founded Ronald McDonald Children's Charities in Canada and Russia. Through these organizations, George has helped to raise money for many children's causes in Canada and in the former Soviet Union.

▶▶▶▶▶▶

## QUICK NOTES

▶ George's outside interests include playing tennis and mountain biking. George also likes to spend time with his two sons and their families.
▶ In 1997, George published his autobiography, *To Russia with Fries*. **Royalties** from the sale of his book go to the Ronald McDonald Children's Charities of Canada.
▶ George has a business card that stands out. Shaped like a Big Mac, the card is good for a free burger at a McDonald's restaurant.
▶ Former Soviet president Mikhail Gorbachev wrote the foreword to George's autobiography.

# Harrison McCain and Wallace McCain

*1927–*

*1930–*

> **"** I remember we worked in the summertime— just as soon as you were old enough to do anything, you worked. You worked in the hayfields, you worked in the fall, picking potatoes. **"**
> Wallace McCain

## Key Events

**1956** Start a food processing business called McCain Foods

**1968** Expand McCain Foods to Britain

**1970** Explore new markets in Australia, Europe, and the United States

**1992** Harrison receives the Companion to the Order of Canada

**1993** Harrison and Wallace are inducted into the Canadian Business Hall of Fame

**1994** Wallace is removed from his top position at McCain Foods

**1995** Wallace takes control of Maple Leaf Foods

**1996** Wallace receives the Order of Canada

**1998** Harrison is awarded a Lifetime Achievement Award from Ernst & Young

# Early Years

**H**arrison and Wallace grew up in New Brunswick, in a small town called Florenceville. They were the two youngest in a family of six children. Harrison was three years older than Wallace. The McCain house was cramped. Harrison and Wallace shared a double bed for many years.

The brothers went to school in a three-room schoolhouse in Florenceville. Most of their friends quit school after the fourth grade so they could help out on their families' farms. Mrs. McCain insisted that her children finish high school and go on to university. Harrison was a self-confident, outgoing boy who did well in school. He loved to read and was good at sports. Wallace also enjoyed sports. He played on the high school hockey team. Unlike his big brother, Wallace was shy and had a hard time in school. His rebellious streak sometimes got Wallace into trouble.

The McCain family believed in hard work. The McCain boys had to earn their own spending money. Harrison sold newspapers on the weekends. Both boys looked after cows on a family farm down the road.

**Older sister Eleanor with Wallace (middle) and Harrison (right).**

## **B**ackgrounder

### The McCains and Potatoes

The McCain family have been potato farmers in and around Florenceville since the 1820s. Harrison and Wallace's father was no exception. A.D. McCain started a successful business in the village in 1909. He sold seed potatoes to local farmers. He also sold seed potatoes to farmers in Cuba and South America. When he died, his wife and his eldest sons, Andrew and Robert, continued to run the family business.

# Developing Skills

**H**arrison studied at Acadia University, Nova Scotia, while Wallace attended Mount Allison University in New Brunswick. Neither brother wanted to go to university, but their parents gave them no choice. After graduating, Harrison and Wallace started working as salesmen. Harrison soon became a sales manager for Irving Oil, owned by K. C. Irving. K. C. Irving was one of the most successful businessmen in New Brunswick. Harrison admired his boss and worked hard at his job. A few years later, Wallace also went to work for K. C. Irving. He became the manager of Irving's wholesale company in New Brunswick.

Harrison decided to go into business for himself, and invited Wallace to join him. But they did not know what kind of business they wanted to do. Their brother Robert told them about an American company that was doing well freezing French fries and peas. They liked the idea, and began looking into starting a similar business in Canada.

Wallace graduated from Mount Allison University when he was twenty-one years old.

# **B**ackgrounder

## K. C. Irving, 1899–1992

K. C. Irving created a huge business empire in New Brunswick. Irving's companies have shaped the province's **economy**. In the 1920s, Irving started his own oil company. He quickly added service stations and garages. Over the years, Irving expanded his business into lumber, transportation, and the media. He became the most powerful businessperson in New Brunswick. By the time he died in 1992, he controlled almost 300 different companies.

In 1956, the McCain brothers decided to start a business to turn New Brunswick potatoes into frozen French fries. They invested money they had inherited from their father and created McCain Foods. The government lent the brothers money to help build a factory in Florenceville. A few months later, the first packages of McCain frozen French fries were ready for sale.

Now, Harrison and Wallace had to convince Canadians to try their new product. Canadians were not as familiar with frozen food as Americans. The fast-food industry had not yet taken hold in Canada. It was a tough sell, but the McCain brothers were good salesmen. They did not give up easily. They travelled across the country telling people about their frozen French fries. When the number of fast-food restaurants started to grow, so did the sales of McCain fries. In just a few years, McCain became the largest frozen food business in Canada.

> **❝** It was all basic sales work. We called at restaurants where they were still cutting their own french fries.... I called on restaurants from one side of the country to the other. **❞**
>
> *Harrison McCain*

# Accomplishments

In the early years of their business, Harrison and Wallace worked without stopping. There were many problems to solve. The brothers worked together to build their business. Their personalities and skills fit well together. Harrison was the overall planner. Wallace looked after the details of the business. Over time, the business started to grow. The brothers increased the number of products, freezing different kinds of vegetables. They bought farmland. They grew seed potatoes. They blended and sold fertilizer. They built equipment to harvest potatoes and other vegetables. They bought a trucking company to ship McCain products.

After years of working with his brother, Harrison now runs McCain Foods without Wallace.

▶▶▶▶▶▶

## Quick Notes

▶ The McCains built their first factory in an old cow pasture, a few hundred metres from their father's produce company office.

▶ In 1994, Wallace McCain's wife, Margaret Norrie McCain, became lieutenant governor of New Brunswick.

▶ To stay competitive, McCain Foods always looks for new ways to prepare and package its products. In the early 1980s, McCain was the first company to use Tetra Paks for its juices. Now, juice boxes are a familiar sight.

▶ Today, you can buy McCain French fries in Japan, Europe, South America, and Australia. McCain sells most of its products outside of Canada.

▶ Harrison has five children and Wallace has four. Many of their children have worked for McCain Foods.

After a time, the brothers wanted to expand their business outside Canada. They avoided the United States in the beginning, because many other companies were already in the frozen food business. They decided to start in Britain, where frozen food was still a novelty. They started by selling frozen peas in Britain. Soon they were selling French fries and other products to the British. With this success, they looked at new markets in Europe and Australia. They later started doing business in the United States. They continued to add new products, such as frozen pizzas and frozen juice.

Their business spread throughout the world, but the McCain head office stayed in Florenceville. Many members of their family worked in the business. The McCains were an important part of New Brunswick. Their business had created many jobs in the province. Harrison and Wallace were well-respected in their home town and in New Brunswick.

By the early 1990s, McCain Foods had become one of the most successful food companies in the world. McCain now has fifty-five factories in eleven countries. More than 6,000 people work for McCain.

After almost forty years in business together, Harrison and Wallace went their separate ways in 1994. They disagreed about who would run the company when they retired. After a bitter legal fight in court, Wallace was asked to leave his top position in the company. Harrison still runs McCain Foods from Florenceville. Wallace has moved to Toronto. He still owns part of McCain, but he now runs Maple Leaf Foods.

> 66 We heard all our lives about exports. Dad sold potatoes in Argentina, Venezuela, Uruguay, and Cuba.... So that was the thing that made us go international. 99
>
> Wallace McCain

In 1995, Wallace McCain left McCain Foods and took control of Maple Leaf Foods.

# Backgrounder

## Family Feud

For many years, the McCain brothers ran their business as a team. They shared the role as head of the company. Their offices sat side by side with a door connecting the two rooms. They talked all the time and made decisions informally. They even lived on the same hill in Florenceville. When the brothers started to disagree about the future of McCain, all this changed. Their disagreement became front-page news across the country. Family members were asked to take sides. Rivalry from childhood days came back to the surface. Long battles in court caused bad feelings between the brothers.

1942–

# Lise Watier

> ❝ When I started, my only capital was myself. I had no money. Nobody around me believed in me. ❞

## Key Events

**1963** Begins career as a television host

**1965** Opens her own beauty school

**1968** Forms the Institut Lise Watier in Montreal

**1972** Begins making and selling her own line of cosmetics

**1990** Rebuilds her business after a fire destroys the head office

**1992** Is named one of Canada's top ten entrepreneurs of the decade by *Profit* magazine

**1993** Launches a new perfume called Neiges

**1998** Is honoured by the Montreal Marketing Association as marketing personality of the year

# Early Years

Lise grew up as an only child in Montreal. Both of her parents were businesspeople. Her father ran a car dealership. Lise's mother worked as a buyer for her sister's clothing store. In those days, it was unusual for a married woman to work outside the home.

Lise learned a great deal from her mother. She visited clothing manufacturers and watched her mother work. She listened to her mother talk about fashion, colour, and style. Lise admired her mother.

As a teenager, Lise was very interested in beauty. She cut her friends' hair and did their makeup. One day, Lise read the life story of Helena Rubinstein, the well-respected beautician and businesswoman. Rubinstein's life inspired Lise. The book showed Lise how she could turn her interest in beauty into her life's work.

When she was young, Lise dreamed of the day she would have her own cosmetics business.

## Backgrounder

### Helena Rubinstein, 1882–1965

Helena was born in Poland. As a young woman, she trained in medicine. In 1902, she moved to Australia and opened her first beauty salon. She used a family recipe for face cream to start her cosmetics empire. She opened beauty salons in London, Paris, and New York City. After World War I, Helena started making and selling cosmetics around the world. When she died in 1965, she was one of the ten richest women in the world.

# Developing Skills

When she was a young woman, Lise started working in television. Her television career happened by accident. One night she went to pick up a friend at a television station in Montreal. Someone had not shown up to do a commercial, and Lise was asked to fill in. That was the first night of a five-year career in television. She interviewed hundreds of women on different programs.

Often, Lise talked to her television guests about beauty and manners. Lise realized that many women were interested in these topics. She decided to make recordings that would answer women's questions. Women could buy her records and teach themselves. Later, Lise decided to open a school offering courses in self-improvement and beauty. She quit her job at the television station. Lise worked full-time to develop her new school. In 1968, she named the school the Institut Lise Watier. Here, beauty professionals offered women beauty services and advice.

Lise covered Expo 67 in Montreal for a television program called *Voici l'expo*.

## Backgrounder

### The Ancient Art of Cosmetics

People have been using creams, powders, and dyes to enhance beauty since ancient times. Egyptians used black **kohl** powder to darken the area around their eyes and **henna** dye to colour their skin. In Europe, cosmetics were widely used until the late 1700s. In 1900, cosmetics made a comeback with French women. Making and selling cosmetics has grown into a huge industry.

After a time, Lise wanted to create her own cosmetics. Many people tried to discourage her from manufacturing cosmetics. It was a competitive industry. Most of the companies in it were large companies with big budgets. Lise persevered. She found a chemist in Montreal who specialized in cosmetics. He taught Lise about ingredients and ways to mix them.

> All kinds of people told me I was crazy to try [a career in manufacturing cosmetics]. They warned me that the competition was too strong and that I couldn't make it.

Lise had no business training and very little money. However, she did know a great deal about women and beauty. She knew women wanted good products at affordable prices. She also knew that because of her television career, people knew and respected her. Lise did her homework. She travelled to Europe and talked to people in the fashion industry. She learned about fashion trends. Lise did not have much money for advertising. She had to sell her products by visiting stores. Lise finally got her break at one of the big department stores in Montreal. The cosmetics manager knew Lise from television and decided to sell Lise's products in the store.

While Lise was building her company she took time to have two daughters: Nathalie (pictured here with Lise) and Marie-Lise.

# Accomplishments

**W**omen liked Lise's products and recommended them to their friends. In Quebec, Watier cosmetics became bestsellers. Lise was successful competing with the large cosmetic companies in her home province. She often updated her products to keep them current and interesting. Lise sold her products in other parts of Canada and abroad. A good economy in central Canada helped the business to grow.

> *To make it in any business, it's not enough to give 100 percent. If that's all you have in you, go work for someone else and give them 100 percent. You have to give 200 percent. That's how it happens. That's what pulls you through.*

By 1990, the strong economy was failing. People were buying fewer products, including cosmetics. Lise had to find ways to keep her business going. During this tough time, disaster struck. In 1990, a fire burned her company headquarters to the ground. It also destroyed all of Lise's products. Lise decided to start again. "I literally rolled up my sleeves and said, 'We're starting over.' I don't know where I got the energy, but we began again."

Lise introduced her line of cosmetics to western Canada in 1984.

## Backgrounder

### Women in Business

Fifty years ago, few Canadian women were in business. Today, that has changed. About 150,000 new businesses start up each year in Canada. More than half of them are started by women. Women run businesses of all kinds and sizes. Some Canadian women operate small businesses of their own. Some women are in charge of the largest corporations in the country.

Lise celebrated her twenty-fifth year in the cosmetics industry in 1997.

▶▶▶▶▶▶

## QUICK NOTES

▶ Lise was awarded the Order of Canada.
▶ Lise has been called Quebec's "queen of perfume."
▶ Lise works with chemists to develop new products.
▶ Lise speaks French, English, Spanish, and Italian.
▶ Lise hosts a daily television show in Quebec focusing on beauty secrets.
▶ Lise has two daughters. One is a lawyer, and one is a business school graduate. Both daughters have become involved in their mother's business.

Lise faced many challenges. Banks did not want to lend her money. Lise had to scrape money together to pay her staff. Eventually, an investor helped the company. Lise was able to get the business back on its feet. She kept developing new products. By late 1993, she was ready to launch a new fragrance called *Neiges*, the French word for snow. It was a big risk. The future of her company rested on the success of Neiges. That Christmas, people bought the perfume in droves. Its success gave Lise and her staff the boost they needed. Today, Neiges is the top-selling perfume in Quebec. Neiges also sells well in Paris and London.

To many Quebeckers, Lise is an icon. As a woman in business, she is considered a pioneer. As a Canadian in the cosmetics industry, she is a rare success. Institut Lise Watier is now a five-storey spa in a wealthy neighbourhood in Montreal. The Institut is the biggest of its kind in North America. Lise sells her products all across North America, in France, and the Middle East. Lise is also dedicated to the 170 people who work for her. Many women have become senior managers in the company. Lise tells people starting their own businesses to believe in themselves so strongly that "no one can make you change your mind."

*1935–*

# Moses Znaimer

> **"** The problem is not too much television. The problem is too much of the same television. **"**

## Key Events

**1948** Emigrates to Canada

**1963** Earns an honours bachelor's degree from McGill University

**1965** Earns a master's degree from Harvard University

**1972** Co-founds Citytv in Toronto

**1984** Starts the MuchMusic video channel

**1986** Starts MusiquePlus video channel in Montreal

**1995** Buys Alberta's public education television station with Chum Limited and Ron Keast Group; launches BRAVO!, a fine arts and culture specialty channel

**1997** Launches Space: The Imagination Station

**1998** Receives the Canadian Association of Broadcasters' Gold Ribbon Award for Broadcast Excellence; launches MuchMoreMusic,CablePulse 22, and MuchaMusica channels

**1999** Launches Star Television and Canadian Learning Television

# Early Years

Moses was born in a small village in Tajikstan, part of the former Soviet Union. When Moses was six, the Znaimers came to Canada. They moved to Montreal's immigrant neighbourhood, St. Urbain Street.

As a boy, Moses was small and scrappy. He felt like an outsider. He learned how to survive by his wits and sometimes with his fists. On occasion, he got into trouble with the police over curfews. When Moses was thirteen, he celebrated his **bar mitzvah**. With the money he received, he bought the family's first television set. In those days, not everyone had a television, and his family was the last to have one in his neighbourhood. Moses was fascinated by television. For him, it was a window to the world.

Education was important to the Znaimer family. Moses's parents worked hard to send Moses to a **parochial** school. There he studied the Bible, Hebrew, and Jewish cultural studies in addition to his regular English classes. When he graduated from high school, Moses won a scholarship to McGill University in Montreal. He studied philosophy and politics. Later, he earned a master's degree in government from Harvard University while on scholarship.

Tajikstan has only one state-owned radio broadcast station and one television station.

## **B**ackgrounder

### The Birth of Television

People first had the idea of transmitting sounds and pictures in the late 1800s. It took fifty years to develop the technology to capture images with a camera and send them to a screen. Regular television broadcasting did not begin until the late 1940s. Some of the first television shows were boxing matches and game shows. A few years later, people could watch a few hours of programming in the evening. By the 1950s, viewers could tune in throughout the day and night to watch a growing number of programs. In the early days of television, there were only a few television stations.

# Developing Skills

**M**oses returned to Canada after graduating from Harvard. He started working for the Canadian Broadcasting Corporation (CBC) in Toronto. Moses worked in radio and television. He and another **producer** created Canada's first national open line phone-in show. *Cross Country Check-Up* invited Canadians to call with their comments on different topics. It is still on the air. Moses also appeared in front of the camera for CBC. He co-hosted and co-produced *Take Thirty* and *The Way It Is*.

In 1967, Moses prepared a documentary series to mark the fiftieth anniversary of the Russian Revolution. The thirteen-part program received excellent reviews. With the success of *Revolution Plus Fifty*, Moses became a shining light in Canadian television.

> **My personal taste has always been to seek out the different... if lots of people are doing something already, nobody needs me to do more of it.**

In the early 1970s, Moses got involved in a different kind of business. He tried being a venture capitalist. A venture capitalist is someone who raises money to invest in often risky business ideas. In 1972, Sruki and Phyllis Switzer asked Moses for help. They wanted to start a local television station in Toronto. Moses joined as one of the founding partners in the new station called Citytv. He became Citytv's president and executive producer.

Growing up with little money, Moses knew he had to work hard to get to the top.

It costs a great deal of money to run a television station, even a local station. In the early days, Moses and his partners had trouble paying their bills. By 1975, Citytv owed more money than it had. Help came from Montreal's Multiple Access Corporation. They hired a media expert. The expert said that Toronto had no local newscast. Citytv decided to fill the need. It created CityPulse News.

Moses and his partners knew it would be difficult to compete with established television stations in Toronto if they just tried to do the same kind of television. They wanted Citytv to stand out as something completely different. Moses hired people to reflect the many ethnic groups in the city. He had people report live from news scenes around the city. Moses chose programs and music that appealed to a younger audience. Many of Citytv's shows were filmed without sets or were shot on the streets. Slowly, more and more people started watching Citytv. Moses became known as a **maverick** and a **visionary**.

> **Revolution—that's the theme of my life.**

During Expo 67, Moses worked with American film director John Ford.

# Backgrounder

## Citytv

Today, many broadcasters imitate the Citytv style. But in the early 1970s, Citytv was unique. The Citytv "look" is stylish and casual. News anchors do not sit behind desks. They walk through the newsroom, showing where and how they work. Reporters tape stories with their own video cameras. Moses coined the term "videographer" for these reporters. Citytv's fashionable Queen Street building has large windows opening onto the street. There are no studios in the ChumCity building. Everyday people are a constant, visible part of Citytv's shows.

# Accomplishments

With the success of Citytv in Toronto, Moses and Chum Limited wanted to expand the business. Cable television gave Moses a chance to start channels that would broadcast across Canada. In 1984, he started Canada's first twenty-four-hour music television station, MuchMusic. Two years later, he started a French-language music station called MusiquePlus.

By the mid-1990s, Moses was ready to start more television stations. These included Canada's first channel devoted to the arts, called Bravo! Before they could start Bravo!, Chum Limited had to apply to a government agency called the CRTC. The CRTC controls who can start new television stations in Canada. The CRTC wants to ensure that all Canadian television stations run a certain number of Canadian programs. Some people were concerned that people who produced rock and roll programming could not produce arts programming. Nevertheless, Moses was given the licence. He eventually won the support of the arts community, who liked what they saw on Bravo!

Moses believes that, with television, the people who tell a story are as important as the story itself.

## Backgrounder

### Bravo!

When Moses introduced Bravo!, his specialty arts channel, people were not sure what to expect. Now it is a huge success. Bravo! gives Canadians the opportunity to see films and specials that are not shown on network stations. Bravo! airs foreign and classic movies, original arts features, and unique specials. It profiles Canadian and international people and events in the art world, and is seen by people all over the world.

> 66 *I'm proud to say I've
> stayed in the saddle by
> force of the power of
> ideas. I have had
> control by being
> nimble and quick.* 99

Moses continued to develop new cable stations in Canada. These included a channel called Space and a twenty-four-hour news station. In 1995, Moses, along with three other men, bought an educational channel from the Alberta government. Recently, he took over creative supervision of a television station in rural Ontario. He changed it into a news, entertainment, and sports channel. With the same three men, Moses took over four other Ontario stations. In all of his local Canadian stations, Moses uses the same approach he used at Citytv.

Recently, Moses expanded his television influence beyond Canada. A Spanish version of MuchMusic was launched in Argentina, called MuchaMusica. A music program called *Jyrki* airs daily in Finland. The Citytv program *Fashion Television* has been a huge success. Audiences in 120 countries, including the United States, France, Iceland, and Vietnam tune in to the half-hour show.

Throughout his career, Moses has promoted television. In 1995, he made a three-hour documentary called *TVTV: The Television Revolution*. In *TVTV*, he says that television is the most important influence in our world. Not everyone agrees with Moses about television. Moses loves to see things in new ways, behind or in front of the camera.

▶▶▶▶▶▶

## QUICK NOTES

▶ Growing up, Moses was known as Moishe. He did not change this Yiddish name to the English version until he went to university.

▶ Moses has long been a collector of antique televisions. He displays his collection at his MZTV Museum in Toronto.

▶ Moses has received several human rights awards.

▶ Moses has also been a successful theatre producer. A few years ago, he produced the thriller *Tamara*. The play was one of the longest-running shows in Los Angeles.

# MORE GREAT CANADIANS

The following pages list a few famous Canadians in business whose stories you may want to read about on your own. Use the Suggested Reading list to learn more about these and other famous Canadians.

*1931–*

## Charles Bronfman

*Corporate Executive and Philanthropist*

Charles grew up in Montreal, a member of the wealthy Bronfman family. Charles's father, Sam, had started a liquor company in the 1920s called Seagrams. Charles eventually joined the family business. In the 1960s, he bought the Montreal Expos baseball team when it was having money problems. Charles has been a strong supporter of Canada. In the 1980s, he started a group to promote Canadian culture and history. This CRB Foundation has produced a series of mini-documentaries for television. Its "Heritage Minutes" look at important events and people from Canada's past. He has also invested in many Israeli businesses. The Israeli branch of his CRB Foundation promotes education and health to Israelis and Palestinians.

*1949–*

## Wayne Clark

*Fashion Designer*

When Wayne was growing up, he dreamed of becoming a fashion designer. He went to the Alberta College of Art for a few years before moving to Ontario. There, Wayne studied fashion design. After he graduated, Wayne travelled to London, England, to work with a fashion company. In London, he also designed costumes for the film *The Romantic Englishwoman* starring Glenda Jackson and Michael Caine. Wayne came back to Toronto and started his own design company in 1989. His designs are popular in Canada and the United States.

**Wayne Clark**

*1943–*

## Michael Cowpland

*Computer Software Executive*

Michael began his engineering studies in his home country of England. He moved to Canada to earn his master's degree and Ph.D. Based in Ottawa, Michael started a company called Mitel with a friend. Mitel manufactured switches that control phone lines. In 1985, Michael left Mitel to start Corel, a computer software company. Corel now has 1,600 employees. The company's drawing software is the leader in its field. Corel continues to be a strong player in the competitive computer industry. Michael himself is fiercely competitive, as a businessman and as a tennis player. In 1995, at age 52, he played in the veteran men's tennis finals at Wimbledon, England.

## Ghermezian Family

*Land Owners and Developers*

The four Ghermezian brothers grew up in Iran. In 1959, they moved to Montreal with their parents. Eskander, Raphael, Nader, Bahman, and their father, Jacob, sold imported carpets from a small shop. Soon, the Ghermezians became the largest carpet distributors in North America. In 1965, the brothers and their families moved to Edmonton. There, they started to buy and develop land. In the 1980s, the Ghermezians were Alberta's largest private owners of city land. In 1981, they opened West Edmonton Mall, the second-largest shopping centre in North America. In 1992, the Ghermezians opened their Mall of America in Minnesota, the largest retail mall in the United States. Successful businessmen, the Ghermezians also support many charities.

*1922–*

## Jack McClelland

*Book Publisher*

In the early 1960s, the Canadian publishing business was small and books by Canadian authors were hard to find. Jack decided to change that. In 1961, he took over his father's publishing company, McClelland & Stewart. He set out to find good Canadian writers and sell their books. Jack started publishing the works of unknown writers. Today, many of them are well-known, such as Margaret Atwood, Mordecai Richler, and Farley Mowat. Running a successful publishing company in Canada was not easy. Jack weathered many hard times. Today, Jack has retired from the business, but McClelland & Stewart is still one of the top publishing companies of Canadian writers.

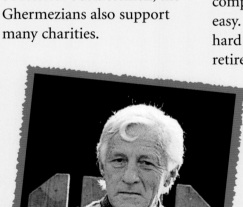

**Jack McClelland**

## 1946–

# Umberto Menghi

*Restaurateur*

Umberto grew up in Florence, Italy. When he was twelve years old, he ran away from home. He washed dishes at an inn and fell in love with restaurants. Umberto set out to learn as much as he could about running a restaurant. He worked in Italy, France, Switzerland, England, and Canada. In 1968, he moved to Vancouver and opened his first restaurant. Since then, Umberto has opened successful restaurants in Vancouver, Whistler, and San Francisco. He has published best-selling cookbooks, and in 1995, he opened a cooking school near his native Florence.

**Umberto Menghi**

## 1936–

# Sylvia Rempel

*Clothing Manufacturer*

In the early 1970s, Sylvia started sewing winter clothes for her children in her Calgary basement. She did not think the ski suits sold in stores were designed for cold western Canadian winters. Word spread about Sylvia's warm and well-designed clothing. In 1978, she started her own company called Sun Ice. The popularity of Sun Ice clothing grew quickly. Athletes liked Sylvia's designs. Sylvia started to supply several Canadian Olympic and national teams. In 1982, Sun Ice was chosen as the official clothing supplier for that year's Canadian expedition to Mount Everest. A few years later, Sylvia's company was given further international exposure. At the 1988 Winter Olympic Games in Calgary, all Canadian athletes, coaches, volunteers, and officials wore Sun Ice outerwear.

## 1948–

# Heather Reisman

*Bookstore Owner and Executive*

In 1997, Heather opened Indigo Books in Ontario. Indigo is a megastore selling books, music, and gifts. Heather started out as a social worker in Montreal. She went into management consulting and ran her own company. Heather was president of a large soft-drink company, Cott Beverages, before turning her attention to books. In the next few years, Heather plans to expand her business across the country.

*1930– 1931–*

## Ron and Marg Southern

*Corporate Executives*

As a girl, Marg lived on a farm and loved to ride horses. Her family could not afford a saddle, so she rode bareback. Marg met Ron when they were in high school in Calgary. In those days, Ron and his father were building a small trailer manufacturing business called ATCO. In 1949, Ron became president. He helped to build ATCO into a large international company that does business around the world. In 1975, Ron and Marg built a centre for horseback riding and jumping. At first, Spruce Meadows was not much more than a stable in the countryside a few kilometres south of Calgary. Today, through their efforts, it has developed into one of the top show-jumping facilities in the world.

*1929–*

## Maurice Strong

*Business Administrator and Environmentalist*

Maurice received his first taste of business by working at a Hudson's Bay Company store in the Arctic. Since then, Maurice has worked in many different businesses, mostly energy and financial companies. Maurice has also had a lifetime interest in international issues, such as developing countries and conservation of the environment. In the 1960s, he helped start Canada's international development agency, CIDA. Through the years, he has held many positions at the United Nations.

*1952–*

## Frank Toskan

*Cosmetics Creator and Manufacturer*

Frank Toskan was a makeup artist and photographer in Toronto. He was frustrated with the poor quality and small range of colours available in cosmetics. In the 1980s, he started to experiment. Frank found a high school chemistry book and asked a university chemistry student for advice. He started mixing colours in his Toronto kitchen. In 1985, Frank and a friend started Make-Up Art Cosmetics, or M.A.C. They started by selling their products to professional makeup artists. News of their products spread by word of mouth. Soon, celebrities such as Madonna and top fashion models were wearing the dramatic colors of M.A.C. cosmetics. By the mid-1990s, Frank's company had grown to 800 employees and was selling $150 million worth of makeup.

**Ron and Marg Southern**

# GLOSSARY

**anti-semitism**: dislike or hatred of Jewish people

**bar mitzvah**: a Jewish ceremony when a thirteen-year-old boy assumes new religious responsibilities

**Cold War**: rivalry between the United States and the Soviet Union that started after World War II and lasted until the 1980s

**delegation**: a group of people representing a country or organization

**ecological**: having to do with plants, animals, and their environment

**economy**: the financial affairs of a city or country

**entrepreneur**: a person who starts and runs a business

**glasnost**: a Russian word meaning "openness." Glasnost was a policy introduced in the Soviet Union in the 1980s, when the country was moving away from communism

**henna**: an orange-red dye made from the leaves of the henna plant; used to colour hair and paint designs on skin

**invest**: to use money to buy into something that is expected to make more money

**kohl**: a dark powder that is used as eyeliner or eye shadow, especially in the Middle East

**maverick**: a person who does not follow society's rules, a rebel

**parochial**: run by a religious group

**perestroika**: a Russian word meaning "restructuring." Perestroika was a policy introduced in the Soviet Union in the 1980s, when the country was moving away from communism

**plumb**: a small weight on the end of a line used to measure the depth of water

**producer**: the person in charge of presenting a television program

**royalties**: a portion of money earned from a publication paid to an author

**visionary**: a person with a talent for foreseeing future trends

# SUGGESTED READING

Bata, Thomas J. *Bata: Shoemaker to the World*. Toronto: Stoddart, 1990.

Cohon, George. *To Russia with Fries*. Toronto: McClelland & Stewart, 1997.

Grescoe, Paul and David Cruise. *The Money Rustlers: Self-made Millionaires of the New West*. Toronto: Viking, 1985.

Newman, Peter C. *Titans: How the New Canadian Establishment Seized Power*. Toronto: Viking, 1998.

Rawlinson, H. Graham and J. L. Granatstein. *The Canadian 100: The 100 Most Influential Canadians of the 20th Century*. Toronto: McArthur & Company, 1997.

Robertson, Heather, ed. *Taking Care of Business: Stories of Canadian Women Entrepreneurs*. Bolton, Ontario: Fenn, 1997.

Siklos, Richard. *Shades of Black: Conrad Black and the World's Fastest Growing Press Empire*. Toronto: Reed Books, 1995.

# INDEX